# Soon To Be Mr. & Mrs.

## Wedding Date:

# Wedding Planner

**WEDDING DATE & TIME:**

**VENUE ADDRESS:**

**BUDGET:**

**OFFICIANT:**

**WEDDING PARTY:**

**NOTES & REMINDERS:**

**TO DO LIST:**

# Wedding Budget Planner

| | TOTAL COST: | DEPOSIT: | REMAINDER: |
|---|---|---|---|
| WEDDING VENUE | | | |
| RECEPTION VENUE | | | |
| FLORIST | | | |
| OFFICIANT | | | |
| CATERER | | | |
| WEDDING CAKE | | | |
| BRIDAL ATTIRE | | | |
| GROOM ATTIRE | | | |
| BRIDAL JEWELRY | | | |
| BRIDESMAID ATTIRE | | | |
| GROOMSMEN ATTIRE | | | |
| HAIR & MAKE UP | | | |
| PHOTOGRAPHER | | | |
| VIDEOGRAPHER | | | |
| DJ SERVICE/ENTERTAINMENT | | | |
| INVITATIONS | | | |
| TRANSPORTATION | | | |
| WEDDING PARTY GIFTS | | | |
| RENTALS | | | |
| HONEYMOON | | | |

# 12 Months Before

| | |
|---|---|
| SET THE DATE | CONSIDER FLORISTS |
| SET YOUR BUDGET | RESEARCH CATERERS |
| CHOOSE YOUR THEME | DECIDE ON OFFICIANT |
| ORGANIZE ENGAGEMENT PARTY | CREATE INITIAL GUEST LIST |
| RESEARCH VENUES | CHOOSE WEDDING PARTY |
| BOOK A WEDDING PLANNER | SHOP FOR WEDDING DRESS |
| RESEARCH PHOTOGRAPHERS | REGISTER WITH GIFT REGISTRY |
| RESEARCH VIDEOGRAPHERS | DISCUSS HONEYMOON IDEAS |
| RESEARCH DJ'S/ENTERTAINMENT | RESEARCH WEDDING RINGS |

THINGS TO REMEMBER:

# 9 Months Before

- FINALIZE GUEST LIST
- ORDER INVITATIONS
- PLAN YOUR RECEPTION
- BOOK PHOTOGRAPHER
- BOOK VIDEOGRAPHER
- BOOK FLORIST
- BOOK DJ/ENTERTAINMENT
- BOOK CATERER
- CHOOSE WEDDING CAKE

- CHOOSE WEDDING GOWN
- ORDER BRIDESMAIDS DRESSES
- RESERVE TUXEDOS
- ARRANGE TRANSPORTATION
- BOOK WEDDING VENUE
- BOOK RECEPTION VENUE
- PLAN HONEYMOON
- BOOK OFFICIANT
- BOOK ROOMS FOR GUESTS

THINGS TO REMEMBER:

# 6 Months Before

ORDER THANK YOU NOTES

REVIEW RECEPTION DETAILS

MAKE APPT FOR DRESS FITTING

CONFIRM BRIDEMAIDS DRESSES

GET MARRIAGE LICENSE

BOOK HAIR/MAKE UP STYLIST

CONFIRM MUSIC SELECTIONS

PLAN BRIDAL SHOWER

PLAN REHEARSAL

SHOP FOR WEDDING RINGS

THINGS TO REMEMBER:

# 3 Months Before

- MAIL OUT INVITATIONS
- MEET WITH OFFICIANT
- BUY GIFTS FOR WEDDING PARTY
- BOOK FINAL GOWN FITTING
- BUY WEDDING BANDS
- PLAN YOUR HAIR STYLE
- PURCHASE SHOES/HEELS
- CONFIRM PASSPORTS ARE VALID

- FINALIZE RECEPTION MENU
- PLAN REHEARSAL DINNER
- CONFIRM ALL BOOKINGS
- APPLY FOR MARRIAGE LICENSE
- CONFIRM MUSIC SELECTIONS
- DRAFT WEDDING VOWS
- CHOOSE YOUR MC
- ARRANGE AIRPORT TRANSFER

THINGS TO REMEMBER:

# 1 Month Before

| | |
|---|---|
| CONFIRM FINAL GUEST COUNT | REHEARSE WEDDING VOWS |
| CONFIRM RECEPTION DETAILS | BOOK MANI-PEDI |
| ATTEND FINAL GOWN FITTING | CONFIRM WITH FLORIST |
| CONFIRM PHOTOGRAPHER | CONFIRM VIDEOGRAPHER |
| WRAP WEDDING PARTY GIFTS | PICK UP BRIDEMAIDS DRESSES |
| CREATE PHOTOGRAPHY SHOT LIST | CREATE WEDDING SCHEDULE |

THINGS TO REMEMBER:

# 1 Week Before

- FINALIZE SEATING PLANS
- MAKE PAYMENTS TO VENDORS
- PACK FOR HONEYMOON
- CONFIRM HOTEL RESERVATIONS
- GIVE SCHEDULE TO PARTY

- DELIVER LICENSE TO OFFICIANT
- CONFIRM WITH BAKERY
- PICK UP WEDDING DRESS
- PICK UP TUXEDOS
- GIVE MUSIC LIST TO DJ

THINGS TO REMEMBER:

# 1 Day Before

GET MANICURE/PEDICURE

ATTEND REHEARSAL DINNER

GET A GOOD NIGHT'S SLEEP!

GIVE GIFTS TO WEDDING PARTY

FINALIZE PACKING

TO DO LIST:

# The Big Day!

- [ ] GET HAIR & MAKE UP DONE
- [ ] HAVE A HEALTHY BREAKFAST
- [ ] ENJOY YOUR BIG DAY!
- [ ] MEET WITH BRIDESMAIDS
- [ ] GIVE RINGS TO BEST MAN

TO DO LIST:

# Wedding Planner

## ENGAGEMENT PARTY:

DATE: _____

LOCATION: _____

TIME: _____

NUMBER OF GUESTS: _____

NOTES:

## BRIDAL SHOWER:

DATE: _____

LOCATION: _____

TIME: _____

NUMBER OF GUESTS: _____

NOTES:

## STAG & DOE PARTY:

DATE: _____

LOCATION: _____

TIME: _____

NUMBER OF GUESTS: _____

NOTES:

# Wedding Party

**MAID/MATRON OF HONOR:**

PHONE: _____    DRESS SIZE: _____    SHOE SIZE: _____

EMAIL: _____

**BRIDESMAID:**

PHONE: _____    DRESS SIZE: _____    SHOE SIZE: _____

EMAIL: _____

**BRIDESMAID #2:**

PHONE: _____    DRESS SIZE: _____    SHOE SIZE: _____

EMAIL: _____

**BRIDESMAID #3:**

PHONE: _____    DRESS SIZE: _____    SHOE SIZE: _____

EMAIL: _____

**BRIDESMAID #4:**

PHONE: _____    DRESS SIZE: _____    SHOE SIZE: _____

EMAIL: _____

NOTES:

# Wedding Party

**BEST MAN:**

PHONE:                          WAIST SIZE:                          SHOE SIZE:

NECK SIZE:                      SLEEVE SIZE:                         JACKET SIZE:

EMAIL:

**GROOMSMEN #1:**

PHONE:                          WAIST SIZE:                          SHOE SIZE:

NECK SIZE:                      SLEEVE SIZE:                         JACKET SIZE:

EMAIL:

**GROOMSMEN #2:**

PHONE:                          WAIST SIZE:                          SHOE SIZE:

NECK SIZE:                      SLEEVE SIZE:                         JACKET SIZE:

EMAIL:

**GROOMSMEN #3:**

PHONE:                          WAIST SIZE:                          SHOE SIZE:

NECK SIZE:                      SLEEVE SIZE:                         JACKET SIZE:

EMAIL:

**GROOMSMEN #4:**

PHONE:                          WAIST SIZE:                          SHOE SIZE:

NECK SIZE:                      SLEEVE SIZE:                         JACKET SIZE:

EMAIL:

# Photographer

**PHOTOGRAPHER:**

PHONE: _____    COMPANY: _____

EMAIL: _____    ADDRESS: _____

_____

**WEDDING PACKAGE OVERVIEW:**

EST PRICE: _____

| **INCLUSIONS:** | YES ✓ | NO ✓ | COST: |
|---|---|---|---|
| ENGAGEMENT SHOOT: | | | |
| PHOTO ALBUMS: | | | |
| FRAMES: | | | |
| PROOFS INCLUDED: | | | |
| NEGATIVES INCLUDED: | | | |
| **TOTAL COST:** | | | |

# Videographer

**VIDEOGRAPHER:**

PHONE:                           COMPANY:

EMAIL:                           ADDRESS:

**WEDDING PACKAGE OVERVIEW:**

EST PRICE:

**INCLUSIONS:**          YES ✓          NO ✓          COST:

DUPLICATES/COPIES:

PHOTO MONTAGE:

MUSIC ADDED:

EDITING:

**TOTAL COST**:

NOTES:

# DJ/Entertainment

**DJ/LIVE BAND/ENTERTAINMENT:**

PHONE: _____     COMPANY: _____

EMAIL: _____     ADDRESS: _____

START TIME: _____     END TIME: _____

**ENTERTAINMENT SERVICE OVERVIEW:**

EST PRICE: _____

| **INCLUSIONS:** | YES ✓ | NO ✓ | COST: |
|---|---|---|---|
| SOUND EQUIPMENT: | | | |
| LIGHTING: | | | |
| SPECIAL EFFECTS: | | | |
| GRATUITIES | | | |

**TOTAL COST:** _____

NOTES:

# Florist

**FLORIST:**

PHONE: _____     COMPANY: _____

EMAIL: _____     ADDRESS: _____

**FLORAL PACKAGE:**

EST PRICE: _____

**INCLUSIONS:**          YES  ✓     NO  ✓     COST:

BRIDAL BOUQUET:

THROW AWAY BOUQUET:

CORSAGES:

CEREMONY FLOWERS

CENTERPIECES

CAKE TOPPER

BOUTONNIERE

**TOTAL COST:**

# Wedding Cake/Baker

PHONE: _____     COMPANY: _____

EMAIL: _____     ADDRESS: _____

**WEDDING CAKE PACKAGE:**

COST: _____     FREE TASTING: _____     DELIVERY FEE: _____

FLAVOR: _____

FILLING: _____

SIZE: _____

SHAPE: _____

COLOR: _____

EXTRAS: _____

**TOTAL COST:** _____

NOTES:

# Transportation Planner

**TO CEREMONY:**     PICK UP TIME:     PICK UP LOCATION:

BRIDE:

GROOM:

BRIDE'S PARENTS:

GROOM'S PARENTS:

BRIDESMAIDS:

GROOMSMEN:

**NOTES:**

**TO RECEPTION:**     PICK UP TIME:     PICK UP LOCATION:

BRIDE & GROOM:

BRIDE'S PARENTS:

GROOM'S PARENTS:

BRIDESMAIDS:

GROOMSMEN:

# Wedding Planner

**BACHELORETTE PARTY:**

DATE: .............................    LOCATION: ...............................

TIME: .............................    NUMBER OF GUESTS: ...............

NOTES:

**BACHELOR PARTY:**

DATE: .............................    LOCATION: ...............................

TIME: .............................    NUMBER OF GUESTS: ...............

NOTES:

**CEREMONY REHEARSAL:**

DATE: .............................    LOCATION: ...............................

TIME: .............................    NUMBER OF GUESTS: ...............

NOTES:

# Wedding Planner

**REHEARSAL DINNER:**

DATE:

LOCATION:

TIME:

NUMBER OF GUESTS:

NOTES:

**RECEPTION:**

DATE:

LOCATION:

TIME:

NUMBER OF GUESTS:

NOTES:

REMINDERS:

# Names & Addresses

**CEREMONY:**

PHONE: _____          CONTACT NAME: _____

EMAIL: _____           ADDRESS: _____

**RECEPTION:**

PHONE: _____          CONTACT NAME: _____

EMAIL: _____           ADDRESS: _____

**OFFICIANT:**

PHONE: _____          CONTACT NAME: _____

EMAIL: _____           ADDRESS: _____

**WEDDING PLANNER:**

PHONE: _____          CONTACT NAME: _____

EMAIL: _____           ADDRESS: _____

**CATERER:**

PHONE: _____          CONTACT NAME: _____

EMAIL: _____           ADDRESS: _____

**FLORIST:**

PHONE: _____          CONTACT NAME: _____

EMAIL: _____           ADDRESS: _____

# Names & Addresses

**BAKERY:**

PHONE: _____    CONTACT NAME: _____

EMAIL: _____    ADDRESS: _____

**BRIDAL SHOP:**

PHONE: _____    CONTACT NAME: _____

EMAIL: _____    ADDRESS: _____

**PHOTOGRAPHER:**

PHONE: _____    CONTACT NAME: _____

EMAIL: _____    ADDRESS: _____

**VIDEOGRAPHER:**

PHONE: _____    CONTACT NAME: _____

EMAIL: _____    ADDRESS: _____

**DJ/ENTERTAINMENT:**

PHONE: _____    CONTACT NAME: _____

EMAIL: _____    ADDRESS: _____

**HAIR/NAIL SALON:**

PHONE: _____    CONTACT NAME: _____

EMAIL: _____    ADDRESS: _____

# Names & Addresses

**MAKE UP ARTIST:**

PHONE: _____          CONTACT NAME: _____

EMAIL: _____          ADDRESS: _____

**RENTALS:**

PHONE: _____          CONTACT NAME: _____

EMAIL: _____          ADDRESS: _____

**HONEYMOON RESORT/HOTEL:**

PHONE: _____          CONTACT NAME: _____

EMAIL: _____          ADDRESS: _____

**TRANSPORTATION SERVICE:**

PHONE: _____          CONTACT NAME: _____

EMAIL: _____          ADDRESS: _____

**NOTES:**

# Caterer Details

**CONTACT INFORMATION:**

PHONE: _____    CONTACT NAME: _____

EMAIL: _____    ADDRESS: _____

**MENU CHOICE #1:**

**MENU CHOICE #2:**

|  | YES ✓ | NO ✓ | COST: |
|---|---|---|---|
| BAR INCLUDED: | | | |
| CORKAGE FEE: | | | |
| HORS D'OEUVRES: | | | |
| TAXES INCLUDED: | | | |
| GRATUITIES INCLUDED: | | | |

# Menu Planner

**HORS D'OEUVRES**

**1st COURSE:**

**2nd COURSE:**

**3rd COURSE:**

**4th COURSE:**

**DESSERT:**

# 1 Week Before

| | THINGS TO DO: | NOTES: |
|---|---|---|
| **MONDAY** | | |
| **TUESDAY** | | |
| **WEDNESDAY** | | |
| **THURSDAY** | | |

REMINDERS & NOTES:

# 1 Week Before

| | THINGS TO DO: | NOTES: |
|---|---|---|
| **FRIDAY** | | |
| **SATURDAY** | | |
| **SUNDAY** | | |

**LEFT TO DO:**

**REMINDERS:**

**NOTES:**

# Wedding Guest List

| NAME: | ADDRESS: | # IN PARTY: | RSVP: ✓ |
|-------|----------|-------------|---------|
|  |  |  |  |
|  |  |  |  |
|  |  |  |  |
|  |  |  |  |
|  |  |  |  |
|  |  |  |  |
|  |  |  |  |
|  |  |  |  |
|  |  |  |  |
|  |  |  |  |
|  |  |  |  |
|  |  |  |  |
|  |  |  |  |
|  |  |  |  |
|  |  |  |  |
|  |  |  |  |
|  |  |  |  |
|  |  |  |  |
|  |  |  |  |

# Wedding Guest List

| NAME: | ADDRESS: | # IN PARTY: | RSVP: ✓ |
|-------|----------|-------------|---------|
|       |          |             |         |
|       |          |             |         |
|       |          |             |         |
|       |          |             |         |
|       |          |             |         |
|       |          |             |         |
|       |          |             |         |
|       |          |             |         |
|       |          |             |         |
|       |          |             |         |
|       |          |             |         |
|       |          |             |         |
|       |          |             |         |
|       |          |             |         |
|       |          |             |         |
|       |          |             |         |
|       |          |             |         |
|       |          |             |         |
|       |          |             |         |

# Wedding Guest List

| NAME: | ADDRESS: | # IN PARTY: | RSVP: ✓ |
|-------|----------|-------------|---------|
|       |          |             |         |
|       |          |             |         |
|       |          |             |         |
|       |          |             |         |
|       |          |             |         |
|       |          |             |         |
|       |          |             |         |
|       |          |             |         |
|       |          |             |         |
|       |          |             |         |
|       |          |             |         |
|       |          |             |         |
|       |          |             |         |
|       |          |             |         |
|       |          |             |         |
|       |          |             |         |
|       |          |             |         |
|       |          |             |         |

# Wedding Guest List

| NAME: | ADDRESS: | # IN PARTY: | RSVP: ✓ |
|-------|----------|-------------|---------|
|       |          |             |         |
|       |          |             |         |
|       |          |             |         |
|       |          |             |         |
|       |          |             |         |
|       |          |             |         |
|       |          |             |         |
|       |          |             |         |
|       |          |             |         |
|       |          |             |         |
|       |          |             |         |
|       |          |             |         |
|       |          |             |         |
|       |          |             |         |
|       |          |             |         |
|       |          |             |         |
|       |          |             |         |
|       |          |             |         |
|       |          |             |         |

# Wedding Guest List

| NAME: | ADDRESS: | # IN PARTY: | RSVP: ✓ |
|-------|----------|-------------|---------|
|       |          |             |         |
|       |          |             |         |
|       |          |             |         |
|       |          |             |         |
|       |          |             |         |
|       |          |             |         |
|       |          |             |         |
|       |          |             |         |
|       |          |             |         |
|       |          |             |         |
|       |          |             |         |
|       |          |             |         |
|       |          |             |         |
|       |          |             |         |
|       |          |             |         |
|       |          |             |         |
|       |          |             |         |
|       |          |             |         |
|       |          |             |         |

# Wedding Guest List

| NAME: | ADDRESS: | # IN PARTY: | RSVP: ✓ |
|-------|----------|-------------|---------|
|       |          |             |         |
|       |          |             |         |
|       |          |             |         |
|       |          |             |         |
|       |          |             |         |
|       |          |             |         |
|       |          |             |         |
|       |          |             |         |
|       |          |             |         |
|       |          |             |         |
|       |          |             |         |
|       |          |             |         |
|       |          |             |         |
|       |          |             |         |
|       |          |             |         |
|       |          |             |         |
|       |          |             |         |
|       |          |             |         |
|       |          |             |         |

# Wedding Guest List

| NAME: | ADDRESS: | # IN PARTY: | RSVP: ✓ |
|---|---|---|---|
| | | | |
| | | | |
| | | | |
| | | | |
| | | | |
| | | | |
| | | | |
| | | | |
| | | | |
| | | | |
| | | | |
| | | | |
| | | | |
| | | | |
| | | | |
| | | | |
| | | | |
| | | | |
| | | | |

# Wedding Guest List

| NAME: | ADDRESS: | # IN PARTY: | RSVP: ✓ |
|-------|----------|-------------|---------|
|       |          |             |         |
|       |          |             |         |
|       |          |             |         |
|       |          |             |         |
|       |          |             |         |
|       |          |             |         |
|       |          |             |         |
|       |          |             |         |
|       |          |             |         |
|       |          |             |         |
|       |          |             |         |
|       |          |             |         |
|       |          |             |         |
|       |          |             |         |
|       |          |             |         |
|       |          |             |         |
|       |          |             |         |
|       |          |             |         |
|       |          |             |         |
|       |          |             |         |

# Wedding Guest List

| NAME: | ADDRESS: | # IN PARTY: | RSVP: ✓ |
|---|---|---|---|
| | | | |
| | | | |
| | | | |
| | | | |
| | | | |
| | | | |
| | | | |
| | | | |
| | | | |
| | | | |
| | | | |
| | | | |
| | | | |
| | | | |
| | | | |
| | | | |
| | | | |
| | | | |
| | | | |

# Wedding Guest List

| NAME: | ADDRESS: | # IN PARTY: | RSVP: ✓ |
|-------|----------|-------------|---------|
|       |          |             |         |
|       |          |             |         |
|       |          |             |         |
|       |          |             |         |
|       |          |             |         |
|       |          |             |         |
|       |          |             |         |
|       |          |             |         |
|       |          |             |         |
|       |          |             |         |
|       |          |             |         |
|       |          |             |         |
|       |          |             |         |
|       |          |             |         |
|       |          |             |         |
|       |          |             |         |
|       |          |             |         |
|       |          |             |         |
|       |          |             |         |
|       |          |             |         |

# Wedding Guest List

| NAME: | ADDRESS: | # IN PARTY: | RSVP: ✓ |
|---|---|---|---|
| | | | |
| | | | |
| | | | |
| | | | |
| | | | |
| | | | |
| | | | |
| | | | |
| | | | |
| | | | |
| | | | |
| | | | |
| | | | |
| | | | |
| | | | |
| | | | |
| | | | |
| | | | |
| | | | |

# Wedding Guest List

| NAME: | ADDRESS: | # IN PARTY: | RSVP: ✓ |
|-------|----------|-------------|---------|
|       |          |             |         |
|       |          |             |         |
|       |          |             |         |
|       |          |             |         |
|       |          |             |         |
|       |          |             |         |
|       |          |             |         |
|       |          |             |         |
|       |          |             |         |
|       |          |             |         |
|       |          |             |         |
|       |          |             |         |
|       |          |             |         |
|       |          |             |         |
|       |          |             |         |
|       |          |             |         |
|       |          |             |         |
|       |          |             |         |
|       |          |             |         |

# Wedding Guest List

| NAME: | ADDRESS: | # IN PARTY: | RSVP: ✓ |
|-------|----------|-------------|---------|
|       |          |             |         |
|       |          |             |         |
|       |          |             |         |
|       |          |             |         |
|       |          |             |         |
|       |          |             |         |
|       |          |             |         |
|       |          |             |         |
|       |          |             |         |
|       |          |             |         |
|       |          |             |         |
|       |          |             |         |
|       |          |             |         |
|       |          |             |         |
|       |          |             |         |
|       |          |             |         |
|       |          |             |         |
|       |          |             |         |
|       |          |             |         |

# Wedding Guest List

| NAME: | ADDRESS: | # IN PARTY: | RSVP: ✓ |
|-------|----------|-------------|---------|
|       |          |             |         |
|       |          |             |         |
|       |          |             |         |
|       |          |             |         |
|       |          |             |         |
|       |          |             |         |
|       |          |             |         |
|       |          |             |         |
|       |          |             |         |
|       |          |             |         |
|       |          |             |         |
|       |          |             |         |
|       |          |             |         |
|       |          |             |         |
|       |          |             |         |
|       |          |             |         |
|       |          |             |         |
|       |          |             |         |
|       |          |             |         |

# Wedding Guest List

| NAME: | ADDRESS: | # IN PARTY: | RSVP: ✓ |
|---|---|---|---|
| | | | |
| | | | |
| | | | |
| | | | |
| | | | |
| | | | |
| | | | |
| | | | |
| | | | |
| | | | |
| | | | |
| | | | |
| | | | |
| | | | |
| | | | |
| | | | |
| | | | |
| | | | |
| | | | |

# Wedding Guest List

| NAME: | ADDRESS: | # IN PARTY: | RSVP: ✓ |
|-------|----------|-------------|---------|
|       |          |             |         |
|       |          |             |         |
|       |          |             |         |
|       |          |             |         |
|       |          |             |         |
|       |          |             |         |
|       |          |             |         |
|       |          |             |         |
|       |          |             |         |
|       |          |             |         |
|       |          |             |         |
|       |          |             |         |
|       |          |             |         |
|       |          |             |         |
|       |          |             |         |
|       |          |             |         |
|       |          |             |         |
|       |          |             |         |

# Wedding Guest List

| NAME: | ADDRESS: | # IN PARTY: | RSVP: ✓ |
|---|---|---|---|
| | | | |
| | | | |
| | | | |
| | | | |
| | | | |
| | | | |
| | | | |
| | | | |
| | | | |
| | | | |
| | | | |
| | | | |
| | | | |
| | | | |
| | | | |
| | | | |
| | | | |
| | | | |

# Wedding Guest List

| NAME: | ADDRESS: | # IN PARTY: | RSVP: ✓ |
|-------|----------|-------------|---------|
|       |          |             |         |
|       |          |             |         |
|       |          |             |         |
|       |          |             |         |
|       |          |             |         |
|       |          |             |         |
|       |          |             |         |
|       |          |             |         |
|       |          |             |         |
|       |          |             |         |
|       |          |             |         |
|       |          |             |         |
|       |          |             |         |
|       |          |             |         |
|       |          |             |         |
|       |          |             |         |
|       |          |             |         |
|       |          |             |         |
|       |          |             |         |

# Wedding Guest List

| NAME: | ADDRESS: | # IN PARTY: | RSVP: ✓ |
|-------|----------|-------------|---------|
|       |          |             |         |
|       |          |             |         |
|       |          |             |         |
|       |          |             |         |
|       |          |             |         |
|       |          |             |         |
|       |          |             |         |
|       |          |             |         |
|       |          |             |         |
|       |          |             |         |
|       |          |             |         |
|       |          |             |         |
|       |          |             |         |
|       |          |             |         |
|       |          |             |         |
|       |          |             |         |
|       |          |             |         |
|       |          |             |         |
|       |          |             |         |
|       |          |             |         |

# Wedding Guest List

| NAME: | ADDRESS: | # IN PARTY: | RSVP: ✓ |
|-------|----------|-------------|---------|
|       |          |             |         |
|       |          |             |         |
|       |          |             |         |
|       |          |             |         |
|       |          |             |         |
|       |          |             |         |
|       |          |             |         |
|       |          |             |         |
|       |          |             |         |
|       |          |             |         |
|       |          |             |         |
|       |          |             |         |
|       |          |             |         |
|       |          |             |         |
|       |          |             |         |
|       |          |             |         |
|       |          |             |         |
|       |          |             |         |
|       |          |             |         |

# Wedding Guest List

| NAME: | ADDRESS: | # IN PARTY: | RSVP: ✓ |
|---|---|---|---|
|  |  |  |  |
|  |  |  |  |
|  |  |  |  |
|  |  |  |  |
|  |  |  |  |
|  |  |  |  |
|  |  |  |  |
|  |  |  |  |
|  |  |  |  |
|  |  |  |  |
|  |  |  |  |
|  |  |  |  |
|  |  |  |  |
|  |  |  |  |
|  |  |  |  |
|  |  |  |  |
|  |  |  |  |
|  |  |  |  |
|  |  |  |  |

# Wedding Guest List

| NAME: | ADDRESS: | # IN PARTY: | RSVP: ✓ |
|-------|----------|-------------|---------|
|       |          |             |         |
|       |          |             |         |
|       |          |             |         |
|       |          |             |         |
|       |          |             |         |
|       |          |             |         |
|       |          |             |         |
|       |          |             |         |
|       |          |             |         |
|       |          |             |         |
|       |          |             |         |
|       |          |             |         |
|       |          |             |         |
|       |          |             |         |
|       |          |             |         |
|       |          |             |         |
|       |          |             |         |
|       |          |             |         |

# Wedding Guest List

| NAME: | ADDRESS: | # IN PARTY: | RSVP: ✓ |
|-------|----------|-------------|---------|
|       |          |             |         |
|       |          |             |         |
|       |          |             |         |
|       |          |             |         |
|       |          |             |         |
|       |          |             |         |
|       |          |             |         |
|       |          |             |         |
|       |          |             |         |
|       |          |             |         |
|       |          |             |         |
|       |          |             |         |
|       |          |             |         |
|       |          |             |         |
|       |          |             |         |
|       |          |             |         |
|       |          |             |         |
|       |          |             |         |
|       |          |             |         |
|       |          |             |         |

# Wedding Guest List

| NAME: | ADDRESS: | # IN PARTY: | RSVP: ✓ |
|-------|----------|-------------|----------|
|       |          |             |          |
|       |          |             |          |
|       |          |             |          |
|       |          |             |          |
|       |          |             |          |
|       |          |             |          |
|       |          |             |          |
|       |          |             |          |
|       |          |             |          |
|       |          |             |          |
|       |          |             |          |
|       |          |             |          |
|       |          |             |          |
|       |          |             |          |
|       |          |             |          |
|       |          |             |          |
|       |          |             |          |
|       |          |             |          |
|       |          |             |          |
|       |          |             |          |

# Wedding Guest List

| NAME: | ADDRESS: | # IN PARTY: | RSVP: ✓ |
|---|---|---|---|
| | | | |
| | | | |
| | | | |
| | | | |
| | | | |
| | | | |
| | | | |
| | | | |
| | | | |
| | | | |
| | | | |
| | | | |
| | | | |
| | | | |
| | | | |
| | | | |
| | | | |
| | | | |
| | | | |

# Wedding Guest List

| NAME: | ADDRESS: | # IN PARTY: | RSVP: ✓ |
|---|---|---|---|
| | | | |
| | | | |
| | | | |
| | | | |
| | | | |
| | | | |
| | | | |
| | | | |
| | | | |
| | | | |
| | | | |
| | | | |
| | | | |
| | | | |
| | | | |
| | | | |
| | | | |
| | | | |
| | | | |

# Wedding Guest List

| NAME: | ADDRESS: | # IN PARTY: | RSVP: ✓ |
|---|---|---|---|
| | | | |
| | | | |
| | | | |
| | | | |
| | | | |
| | | | |
| | | | |
| | | | |
| | | | |
| | | | |
| | | | |
| | | | |
| | | | |
| | | | |
| | | | |
| | | | |
| | | | |
| | | | |
| | | | |

# Wedding Guest List

| NAME: | ADDRESS: | # IN PARTY: | RSVP: ✓ |
|---|---|---|---|
| | | | |
| | | | |
| | | | |
| | | | |
| | | | |
| | | | |
| | | | |
| | | | |
| | | | |
| | | | |
| | | | |
| | | | |
| | | | |
| | | | |
| | | | |
| | | | |
| | | | |
| | | | |
| | | | |

# Wedding Guest List

| NAME: | ADDRESS: | # IN PARTY: | RSVP: ✓ |
|-------|----------|-------------|---------|
|       |          |             |         |
|       |          |             |         |
|       |          |             |         |
|       |          |             |         |
|       |          |             |         |
|       |          |             |         |
|       |          |             |         |
|       |          |             |         |
|       |          |             |         |
|       |          |             |         |
|       |          |             |         |
|       |          |             |         |
|       |          |             |         |
|       |          |             |         |
|       |          |             |         |
|       |          |             |         |
|       |          |             |         |
|       |          |             |         |

# Wedding Guest List

| NAME: | ADDRESS: | # IN PARTY: | RSVP: ✓ |
|-------|----------|-------------|---------|
|       |          |             |         |
|       |          |             |         |
|       |          |             |         |
|       |          |             |         |
|       |          |             |         |
|       |          |             |         |
|       |          |             |         |
|       |          |             |         |
|       |          |             |         |
|       |          |             |         |
|       |          |             |         |
|       |          |             |         |
|       |          |             |         |
|       |          |             |         |
|       |          |             |         |
|       |          |             |         |
|       |          |             |         |
|       |          |             |         |
|       |          |             |         |
|       |          |             |         |

# Wedding Guest List

| NAME: | ADDRESS: | # IN PARTY: | RSVP: ✓ |
|---|---|---|---|
| | | | |
| | | | |
| | | | |
| | | | |
| | | | |
| | | | |
| | | | |
| | | | |
| | | | |
| | | | |
| | | | |
| | | | |
| | | | |
| | | | |
| | | | |
| | | | |
| | | | |
| | | | |
| | | | |

# Wedding Guest List

| NAME: | ADDRESS: | # IN PARTY: | RSVP: ✓ |
|-------|----------|-------------|---------|
|       |          |             |         |
|       |          |             |         |
|       |          |             |         |
|       |          |             |         |
|       |          |             |         |
|       |          |             |         |
|       |          |             |         |
|       |          |             |         |
|       |          |             |         |
|       |          |             |         |
|       |          |             |         |
|       |          |             |         |
|       |          |             |         |
|       |          |             |         |
|       |          |             |         |
|       |          |             |         |
|       |          |             |         |
|       |          |             |         |
|       |          |             |         |

# Wedding Guest List

| NAME: | ADDRESS: | # IN PARTY: | RSVP: ✓ |
|---|---|---|---|
| | | | |
| | | | |
| | | | |
| | | | |
| | | | |
| | | | |
| | | | |
| | | | |
| | | | |
| | | | |
| | | | |
| | | | |
| | | | |
| | | | |
| | | | |
| | | | |
| | | | |
| | | | |
| | | | |

# Wedding Guest List

| NAME: | ADDRESS: | # IN PARTY: | RSVP: ✓ |
|-------|----------|-------------|---------|
|       |          |             |         |
|       |          |             |         |
|       |          |             |         |
|       |          |             |         |
|       |          |             |         |
|       |          |             |         |
|       |          |             |         |
|       |          |             |         |
|       |          |             |         |
|       |          |             |         |
|       |          |             |         |
|       |          |             |         |
|       |          |             |         |
|       |          |             |         |
|       |          |             |         |
|       |          |             |         |
|       |          |             |         |
|       |          |             |         |
|       |          |             |         |
|       |          |             |         |

# Wedding Guest List

| NAME: | ADDRESS: | # IN PARTY: | RSVP: ✓ |
|-------|----------|-------------|---------|
|  |  |  |  |
|  |  |  |  |
|  |  |  |  |
|  |  |  |  |
|  |  |  |  |
|  |  |  |  |
|  |  |  |  |
|  |  |  |  |
|  |  |  |  |
|  |  |  |  |
|  |  |  |  |
|  |  |  |  |
|  |  |  |  |
|  |  |  |  |
|  |  |  |  |
|  |  |  |  |
|  |  |  |  |
|  |  |  |  |
|  |  |  |  |

# Wedding Guest List

| NAME: | ADDRESS: | # IN PARTY: | RSVP: ✓ |
|-------|----------|-------------|---------|
|       |          |             |         |
|       |          |             |         |
|       |          |             |         |
|       |          |             |         |
|       |          |             |         |
|       |          |             |         |
|       |          |             |         |
|       |          |             |         |
|       |          |             |         |
|       |          |             |         |
|       |          |             |         |
|       |          |             |         |
|       |          |             |         |
|       |          |             |         |
|       |          |             |         |
|       |          |             |         |
|       |          |             |         |
|       |          |             |         |
|       |          |             |         |

# Wedding Guest List

| NAME: | ADDRESS: | # IN PARTY: | RSVP: ✓ |
|---|---|---|---|
| | | | |
| | | | |
| | | | |
| | | | |
| | | | |
| | | | |
| | | | |
| | | | |
| | | | |
| | | | |
| | | | |
| | | | |
| | | | |
| | | | |
| | | | |
| | | | |
| | | | |
| | | | |
| | | | |

# Wedding Guest List

| NAME: | ADDRESS: | # IN PARTY: | RSVP: ✓ |
|-------|----------|-------------|---------|
|       |          |             |         |
|       |          |             |         |
|       |          |             |         |
|       |          |             |         |
|       |          |             |         |
|       |          |             |         |
|       |          |             |         |
|       |          |             |         |
|       |          |             |         |
|       |          |             |         |
|       |          |             |         |
|       |          |             |         |
|       |          |             |         |
|       |          |             |         |
|       |          |             |         |
|       |          |             |         |
|       |          |             |         |
|       |          |             |         |
|       |          |             |         |
|       |          |             |         |

# Wedding Guest List

| NAME: | ADDRESS: | # IN PARTY: | RSVP: ✓ |
|---|---|---|---|
|  |  |  |  |
|  |  |  |  |
|  |  |  |  |
|  |  |  |  |
|  |  |  |  |
|  |  |  |  |
|  |  |  |  |
|  |  |  |  |
|  |  |  |  |
|  |  |  |  |
|  |  |  |  |
|  |  |  |  |
|  |  |  |  |
|  |  |  |  |
|  |  |  |  |
|  |  |  |  |
|  |  |  |  |
|  |  |  |  |

# Wedding Guest List

| NAME: | ADDRESS: | # IN PARTY: | RSVP: ✓ |
|-------|----------|-------------|---------|
|       |          |             |         |
|       |          |             |         |
|       |          |             |         |
|       |          |             |         |
|       |          |             |         |
|       |          |             |         |
|       |          |             |         |
|       |          |             |         |
|       |          |             |         |
|       |          |             |         |
|       |          |             |         |
|       |          |             |         |
|       |          |             |         |
|       |          |             |         |
|       |          |             |         |
|       |          |             |         |
|       |          |             |         |
|       |          |             |         |
|       |          |             |         |

# Wedding Guest List

| NAME: | ADDRESS: | # IN PARTY: | RSVP: ✓ |
|-------|----------|-------------|---------|
|       |          |             |         |
|       |          |             |         |
|       |          |             |         |
|       |          |             |         |
|       |          |             |         |
|       |          |             |         |
|       |          |             |         |
|       |          |             |         |
|       |          |             |         |
|       |          |             |         |
|       |          |             |         |
|       |          |             |         |
|       |          |             |         |
|       |          |             |         |
|       |          |             |         |
|       |          |             |         |
|       |          |             |         |
|       |          |             |         |

# Wedding Guest List

| NAME: | ADDRESS: | # IN PARTY: | RSVP: ✓ |
|-------|----------|-------------|---------|
|       |          |             |         |
|       |          |             |         |
|       |          |             |         |
|       |          |             |         |
|       |          |             |         |
|       |          |             |         |
|       |          |             |         |
|       |          |             |         |
|       |          |             |         |
|       |          |             |         |
|       |          |             |         |
|       |          |             |         |
|       |          |             |         |
|       |          |             |         |
|       |          |             |         |
|       |          |             |         |
|       |          |             |         |
|       |          |             |         |

# Wedding Guest List

| NAME: | ADDRESS: | # IN PARTY: | RSVP: ✓ |
|-------|----------|-------------|---------|
|       |          |             |         |
|       |          |             |         |
|       |          |             |         |
|       |          |             |         |
|       |          |             |         |
|       |          |             |         |
|       |          |             |         |
|       |          |             |         |
|       |          |             |         |
|       |          |             |         |
|       |          |             |         |
|       |          |             |         |
|       |          |             |         |
|       |          |             |         |
|       |          |             |         |
|       |          |             |         |
|       |          |             |         |
|       |          |             |         |
|       |          |             |         |

# Wedding Guest List

| NAME: | ADDRESS: | # IN PARTY: | RSVP: ✓ |
|-------|----------|-------------|---------|
|       |          |             |         |
|       |          |             |         |
|       |          |             |         |
|       |          |             |         |
|       |          |             |         |
|       |          |             |         |
|       |          |             |         |
|       |          |             |         |
|       |          |             |         |
|       |          |             |         |
|       |          |             |         |
|       |          |             |         |
|       |          |             |         |
|       |          |             |         |
|       |          |             |         |
|       |          |             |         |
|       |          |             |         |
|       |          |             |         |
|       |          |             |         |

# Wedding Guest List

| NAME: | ADDRESS: | # IN PARTY: | RSVP: ✓ |
|-------|----------|-------------|---------|
|       |          |             |         |
|       |          |             |         |
|       |          |             |         |
|       |          |             |         |
|       |          |             |         |
|       |          |             |         |
|       |          |             |         |
|       |          |             |         |
|       |          |             |         |
|       |          |             |         |
|       |          |             |         |
|       |          |             |         |
|       |          |             |         |
|       |          |             |         |
|       |          |             |         |
|       |          |             |         |
|       |          |             |         |
|       |          |             |         |

# Wedding Guest List

| NAME: | ADDRESS: | # IN PARTY: | RSVP: ✓ |
|---|---|---|---|
| | | | |
| | | | |
| | | | |
| | | | |
| | | | |
| | | | |
| | | | |
| | | | |
| | | | |
| | | | |
| | | | |
| | | | |
| | | | |
| | | | |
| | | | |
| | | | |
| | | | |
| | | | |
| | | | |

# Wedding Guest List

| NAME: | ADDRESS: | # IN PARTY: | RSVP: ✓ |
|---|---|---|---|
| | | | |
| | | | |
| | | | |
| | | | |
| | | | |
| | | | |
| | | | |
| | | | |
| | | | |
| | | | |
| | | | |
| | | | |
| | | | |
| | | | |
| | | | |
| | | | |
| | | | |
| | | | |
| | | | |

# Wedding Guest List

| NAME: | ADDRESS: | # IN PARTY: | RSVP: ✓ |
|---|---|---|---|
| | | | |
| | | | |
| | | | |
| | | | |
| | | | |
| | | | |
| | | | |
| | | | |
| | | | |
| | | | |
| | | | |
| | | | |
| | | | |
| | | | |
| | | | |
| | | | |
| | | | |
| | | | |
| | | | |

# Wedding Guest List

| NAME: | ADDRESS: | # IN PARTY: | RSVP: ✓ |
|---|---|---|---|
| | | | |
| | | | |
| | | | |
| | | | |
| | | | |
| | | | |
| | | | |
| | | | |
| | | | |
| | | | |
| | | | |
| | | | |
| | | | |
| | | | |
| | | | |
| | | | |
| | | | |
| | | | |
| | | | |

# Wedding Guest List

| NAME: | ADDRESS: | # IN PARTY: | RSVP: ✓ |
|-------|----------|-------------|---------|
|       |          |             |         |
|       |          |             |         |
|       |          |             |         |
|       |          |             |         |
|       |          |             |         |
|       |          |             |         |
|       |          |             |         |
|       |          |             |         |
|       |          |             |         |
|       |          |             |         |
|       |          |             |         |
|       |          |             |         |
|       |          |             |         |
|       |          |             |         |
|       |          |             |         |
|       |          |             |         |
|       |          |             |         |
|       |          |             |         |
|       |          |             |         |
|       |          |             |         |

# Wedding Guest List

| NAME: | ADDRESS: | # IN PARTY: | RSVP: ✓ |
|---|---|---|---|
|  |  |  |  |
|  |  |  |  |
|  |  |  |  |
|  |  |  |  |
|  |  |  |  |
|  |  |  |  |
|  |  |  |  |
|  |  |  |  |
|  |  |  |  |
|  |  |  |  |
|  |  |  |  |
|  |  |  |  |
|  |  |  |  |
|  |  |  |  |
|  |  |  |  |
|  |  |  |  |
|  |  |  |  |
|  |  |  |  |
|  |  |  |  |

# Wedding Guest List

| NAME: | ADDRESS: | # IN PARTY: | RSVP: ✓ |
|---|---|---|---|
| | | | |
| | | | |
| | | | |
| | | | |
| | | | |
| | | | |
| | | | |
| | | | |
| | | | |
| | | | |
| | | | |
| | | | |
| | | | |
| | | | |
| | | | |
| | | | |
| | | | |
| | | | |
| | | | |

# Wedding Guest List

| NAME: | ADDRESS: | # IN PARTY: | RSVP: ✓ |
|-------|----------|-------------|---------|
|       |          |             |         |
|       |          |             |         |
|       |          |             |         |
|       |          |             |         |
|       |          |             |         |
|       |          |             |         |
|       |          |             |         |
|       |          |             |         |
|       |          |             |         |
|       |          |             |         |
|       |          |             |         |
|       |          |             |         |
|       |          |             |         |
|       |          |             |         |
|       |          |             |         |
|       |          |             |         |
|       |          |             |         |
|       |          |             |         |
|       |          |             |         |

# Wedding Guest List

| NAME: | ADDRESS: | # IN PARTY: | RSVP: ✓ |
|---|---|---|---|
| | | | |
| | | | |
| | | | |
| | | | |
| | | | |
| | | | |
| | | | |
| | | | |
| | | | |
| | | | |
| | | | |
| | | | |
| | | | |
| | | | |
| | | | |
| | | | |
| | | | |
| | | | |
| | | | |

# Wedding Guest List

| NAME: | ADDRESS: | # IN PARTY: | RSVP: ✓ |
|-------|----------|-------------|---------|
|       |          |             |         |
|       |          |             |         |
|       |          |             |         |
|       |          |             |         |
|       |          |             |         |
|       |          |             |         |
|       |          |             |         |
|       |          |             |         |
|       |          |             |         |
|       |          |             |         |
|       |          |             |         |
|       |          |             |         |
|       |          |             |         |
|       |          |             |         |
|       |          |             |         |
|       |          |             |         |
|       |          |             |         |
|       |          |             |         |

# Wedding Guest List

| NAME: | ADDRESS: | # IN PARTY: | RSVP: ✓ |
|-------|----------|-------------|---------|
|       |          |             |         |
|       |          |             |         |
|       |          |             |         |
|       |          |             |         |
|       |          |             |         |
|       |          |             |         |
|       |          |             |         |
|       |          |             |         |
|       |          |             |         |
|       |          |             |         |
|       |          |             |         |
|       |          |             |         |
|       |          |             |         |
|       |          |             |         |
|       |          |             |         |
|       |          |             |         |
|       |          |             |         |
|       |          |             |         |
|       |          |             |         |
|       |          |             |         |

# Wedding Guest List

| NAME: | ADDRESS: | # IN PARTY: | RSVP: ✓ |
|---|---|---|---|
| | | | |
| | | | |
| | | | |
| | | | |
| | | | |
| | | | |
| | | | |
| | | | |
| | | | |
| | | | |
| | | | |
| | | | |
| | | | |
| | | | |
| | | | |
| | | | |
| | | | |
| | | | |
| | | | |

# Wedding Guest List

| NAME: | ADDRESS: | # IN PARTY: | RSVP: ✓ |
|-------|----------|-------------|---------|
|       |          |             |         |
|       |          |             |         |
|       |          |             |         |
|       |          |             |         |
|       |          |             |         |
|       |          |             |         |
|       |          |             |         |
|       |          |             |         |
|       |          |             |         |
|       |          |             |         |
|       |          |             |         |
|       |          |             |         |
|       |          |             |         |
|       |          |             |         |
|       |          |             |         |
|       |          |             |         |
|       |          |             |         |
|       |          |             |         |
|       |          |             |         |

# Wedding Guest List

| NAME: | ADDRESS: | # IN PARTY: | RSVP: ✓ |
|---|---|---|---|
|  |  |  |  |
|  |  |  |  |
|  |  |  |  |
|  |  |  |  |
|  |  |  |  |
|  |  |  |  |
|  |  |  |  |
|  |  |  |  |
|  |  |  |  |
|  |  |  |  |
|  |  |  |  |
|  |  |  |  |
|  |  |  |  |
|  |  |  |  |
|  |  |  |  |
|  |  |  |  |
|  |  |  |  |
|  |  |  |  |
|  |  |  |  |

# Wedding Guest List

| NAME: | ADDRESS: | # IN PARTY: | RSVP: ✓ |
|-------|----------|-------------|---------|
|       |          |             |         |
|       |          |             |         |
|       |          |             |         |
|       |          |             |         |
|       |          |             |         |
|       |          |             |         |
|       |          |             |         |
|       |          |             |         |
|       |          |             |         |
|       |          |             |         |
|       |          |             |         |
|       |          |             |         |
|       |          |             |         |
|       |          |             |         |
|       |          |             |         |
|       |          |             |         |
|       |          |             |         |
|       |          |             |         |

# Wedding Guest List

| NAME: | ADDRESS: | # IN PARTY: | RSVP: ✓ |
|---|---|---|---|
| | | | |
| | | | |
| | | | |
| | | | |
| | | | |
| | | | |
| | | | |
| | | | |
| | | | |
| | | | |
| | | | |
| | | | |
| | | | |
| | | | |
| | | | |
| | | | |
| | | | |
| | | | |
| | | | |

# Wedding Guest List

| NAME: | ADDRESS: | # IN PARTY: | RSVP: ✓ |
|---|---|---|---|
| | | | |
| | | | |
| | | | |
| | | | |
| | | | |
| | | | |
| | | | |
| | | | |
| | | | |
| | | | |
| | | | |
| | | | |
| | | | |
| | | | |
| | | | |
| | | | |
| | | | |
| | | | |
| | | | |

# Seating Chart Planner

Table #

Table #

Table #

Table #

SEATING PLANNER NOTES:

# Seating Chart Planner

Table #

Table #

Table #

Table #

SEATING PLANNER NOTES:

# Seating Chart Planner

Table #

Table #

Table #

Table #

SEATING PLANNER NOTES:

# Seating Chart Planner

Table #

Table #

Table #

Table #

SEATING PLANNER NOTES:

# Seating Chart Planner

Table #

Table #

Table #

Table #

SEATING PLANNER NOTES:

# Seating Chart Planner

Table #

Table #

Table #

Table #

SEATING PLANNER NOTES:

# Seating Chart Planner

Table #

Table #

Table #

Table #

SEATING PLANNER NOTES:

# Seating Chart Planner

Table #

Table #

Table #

Table #

SEATING PLANNER NOTES:

# Seating Chart Planner

Table #

Table #

Table #

Table #

SEATING PLANNER NOTES:

# Seating Chart Planner

Table #

Table #

Table #

Table #

SEATING PLANNER NOTES:

# Seating Chart Planner

Table #

Table #

Table #

Table #

SEATING PLANNER NOTES:

# Seating Chart Planner

Table #

Table #

Table #

Table #

SEATING PLANNER NOTES:

# Seating Chart Planner

Table #

Table #

Table #

Table #

SEATING PLANNER NOTES:

# Seating Chart Planner

Table #

Table #

Table #

Table #

SEATING PLANNER NOTES:

# Seating Chart Planner

Table #

Table #

Table #

Table #

SEATING PLANNER NOTES:

# Seating Chart Planner

Table #

Table #

Table #

Table #

SEATING PLANNER NOTES:

# Seating Chart Planner

Table #

Table #

Table #

Table #

SEATING PLANNER NOTES:

# Seating Chart Planner

Table #

Table #

Table #

Table #

SEATING PLANNER NOTES:

# Seating Chart Planner

Table #

Table #

Table #

Table #

SEATING PLANNER NOTES:

# Seating Chart Planner

Table #

Table #

Table #

Table #

SEATING PLANNER NOTES:

# Seating Chart Planner

Table #

Table #

Table #

Table #

SEATING PLANNER NOTES:

# Seating Chart Planner

Table #

Table #

Table #

Table #

SEATING PLANNER NOTES:

# Seating Chart Planner

Table #

Table #

Table #

Table #

SEATING PLANNER NOTES:

# Seating Chart Planner

Table #

Table #

Table #

Table #

SEATING PLANNER NOTES:

# Seating Chart Planner

Table #

Table #

Table #

Table #

SEATING PLANNER NOTES:

# Seating Chart Planner

Table #

Table #

Table #

Table #

SEATING PLANNER NOTES:

# Seating Chart Planner

Table #

Table #

Table #

Table #

SEATING PLANNER NOTES:

# Seating Chart Planner

Table #

Table #

Table #

Table #

SEATING PLANNER NOTES:

# Seating Chart Planner

Table #

Table #

Table #

Table #

SEATING PLANNER NOTES:

# Seating Chart Planner

Table #

Table #

Table #

Table #

SEATING PLANNER NOTES:

# Seating Chart Planner

Table #

Table #

Table #

Table #

SEATING PLANNER NOTES:

# Seating Chart Planner

Table #

Table #

Table #

Table #

SEATING PLANNER NOTES:

# Seating Chart Planner

Table #

Table #

Table #

Table #

SEATING PLANNER NOTES:

# Seating Chart Planner

Table #

Table #

Table #

Table #

SEATING PLANNER NOTES:

# Seating Chart Planner

Table #

Table #

Table #

Table #

SEATING PLANNER NOTES:

# Seating Chart Planner

Table #

Table #

Table #

Table #

SEATING PLANNER NOTES:

# Seating Chart Planner

Table #

Table #

Table #

Table #

SEATING PLANNER NOTES:

# Seating Chart Planner

Table #

Table #

Table #

Table #

SEATING PLANNER NOTES:

# Seating Chart Planner

Table #

Table #

Table #

Table #

SEATING PLANNER NOTES:

# Seating Chart Planner

Table #

Table #

Table #

Table #

SEATING PLANNER NOTES:

# Seating Chart Planner

Table #

Table #

Table #

Table #

SEATING PLANNER NOTES:

# Seating Chart Planner

Table #

Table #

Table #

Table #

SEATING PLANNER NOTES:

# Seating Chart Planner

Table #

Table #

Table #

Table #

SEATING PLANNER NOTES:

# Seating Chart Planner

Table #

Table #

Table #

Table #

SEATING PLANNER NOTES:

# Seating Chart Planner

Table #

Table #

Table #

Table #

SEATING PLANNER NOTES:

# Seating Chart Planner

Table #

Table #

Table #

Table #

SEATING PLANNER NOTES:

# Seating Chart Planner

Table #

Table #

Table #

Table #

SEATING PLANNER NOTES:

# Seating Chart Planner

Table #

Table #

Table #

Table #

SEATING PLANNER NOTES:

# Seating Chart Planner

Table #

Table #

Table #

Table #

SEATING PLANNER NOTES:

# Seating Chart Planner

Table #

Table #

Table #

Table #

SEATING PLANNER NOTES:

# Seating Chart Planner

Table #

Table #

Table #

Table #

SEATING PLANNER NOTES:

# Seating Chart Planner

Table #

Table #

Table #

Table #

SEATING PLANNER NOTES:

# Seating Chart Planner

Table #

Table #

Table #

Table #

SEATING PLANNER NOTES:

# Seating Chart Planner

Table #

Table #

Table #

Table #

SEATING PLANNER NOTES:

# Seating Chart Planner

Table #

Table #

Table #

Table #

SEATING PLANNER NOTES:

# Seating Chart Planner

Table #

Table #

Table #

Table #

SEATING PLANNER NOTES:

# Seating Chart Planner

Table #

Table #

Table #

Table #

SEATING PLANNER NOTES:

# Seating Chart Planner

Table #

Table #

Table #

Table #

SEATING PLANNER NOTES:

Made in the USA
Coppell, TX
24 June 2022

79211663R00083